Poland

Adam Bujak

To my Mother

Adam Bujak

Poland

Adam Bujak

BOSZ

Introduction
ks. Jan Twardowski

Text
Anna Szczucka

Translation
Teresa Bałuk-Ulewiczowa

Design
Władysław Pluta

Editor
Joanna Kułakowska-Lis

DTP
Inter Line, Kraków

Prepress
JML, Jacek Jutrzenka

Print and binding
Gorenjski Tisk, Kranj – Slovenija

Wydawnictwo BOSZ
Olszanica 2006

ISBN
83-87730-17-3

Publisher
BOSZ
38-622 Olszanica 311; Office: 38-600 Lesko, ul. Parkowa 5
tel. +48 (13) 4699000, fax +48 (13) 4696188
e-mail: biuro@bosz.com.pl
www.bosz.com.pl

Contents

Introduction
6

Strongholds
74

Folklore
166

Landscapes
10

Residences
110

Churches
206

Symbols
52

Cities
138

Graves
242

Introduction

This album, entitled *Poland*, by Adam Bujak, is testimony enclosed in photographic pictures to the grand distinctiveness of the Polish nation, as manifest in its culture, history, art, religion, and customs. It shows those components which make up the distinctiveness of the society that inhabits this land, rich with the experiences of its shared history and customs. The attributes which set Polish society apart from others are the qualities which go to make the nation's genius: its longing for freedom and social independence, its need of tolerance and hospitality to strangers, and its loyalty to allies. Thanks to these qualities there have been so many moments in Poland's history of glory, so many reasons for pride. In Poland not the governors but the governed have determined the nature of their laws – from the articles Henri de Valois agreed to in 1573 when he was elected monarch, thereby defining the constitutional principles the Polish state would be governed by; through the Third of May Constitution of 1791, Europe's first fully-fledged constitution founded on the principles of statehood put forward by the Enlightenment. The people of Poland have never tolerated the notion of others deciding their fate for them. That is why in the 1980's the Solidarity social and political movement, with its distinctively pluralist and democratic character, evoked such strong, widescale and resolute support. For above all the Polish nation loves freedom, and throughout its long history has given many a proof of the heroism with which it can fight for its freedom. At the same time for many centuries Poland has prided herself on her tolerance to other nations, religions, and ideas. Although strife and conflicts did occur, they cannot obfuscate the beautiful record of a country which welcomed within its borders strangers fleeing persecution on grounds of religion or ideas. We should not forget the noble gestures of reconciliation which came even in the last, difficult times of a debilitated Communism and in tense political situations. An example is the 1989 Round Table, at which a programme of evolving change in Poland's political and economic system was negotiated, and which has become a household name in a uniting Europe. Poles have never oppressed the vanquished; nor downtrodden those weaker than themselves; they strove to achieve understanding and concord.

Their loyalty to allies, not always based on grounds of reason – to Napoleon when they were deprived of sovereignty, and to Britain during the Second World War – bears witness to their noble-mindedness, but also to an idealism their idealised allies did not always reciprocate. We are moved by the motto 'For your freedom and for our freedom' associated with the best traditions of Poland's struggles for liberty, and invigorated in the times when Poles fought in foreign lands and under foreign banners. Tadeusz Kościuszko and Kazimierz Pułaski, who crossed the ocean to offer their heroism and military skills to the young American nation in its bid for freedom, entered world history through such deeds.

In these photographs by Adam Bujak not only may the spirit of the Polish nation be observed, but also the greatness of its local patriotism and the beauty of its regions and localities. In this album its creator may be admired not only for his skill, but also for his love of his country and loving approach to its presentation. The distinguished photographer shows us Poland's people, cultural monuments, religious art, events, and finally her graveyards. There is a well-known saying, 'A nation which loses its remembrance loses its life.' Although cemeteries speak of those who have died, they preserve a nation's life and give us the opportunity of seeing those who have escaped the gaze of our eyes.

This album is full of a loving, warm-hearted, patient and persistent, blessed and reverent remembrance. It permits us to observe the fullness of that country's beauty and grandeur. And it substantiates the Polish nation's sense of self-esteem, helping to rediscover its place in history and in the present-day.

Father Jan Twardowski

Poland

Situation: in Central Europe, on the Baltic Sea

Surface area: 312,685 sq. km

Climate: temperate zone

Population: approx. 39 million

Official language: Polish

Form of government: parliamentary republic

Currency: Polish złoty = 100 groszy

Flag: red-and-white

Emblem: the Crowned White Eagle, on red background

Capital: Warsaw, population 1.6 million

Landscapes

What is Poland actually like? You cannot show her beauty in a single tableau. There is no typically Polish landscape, at the sight of which you can say, 'Yes, this is Poland.' If that picture happened to be a mountain scene, you'd ask, 'Where's the sea? Where are the lakes? Where the willows of Mazovia? Where the beach along the coastline?' And then, to complete the picture, you would ask again for the hills and mountains... That's what Poland is like, one in plurality; everywhere in Poland you'll find something unique, something delightful, nostalgic, joyous, different from any other place in the world.

Her varying climate and the diversity of her landscapes make Poland virtually self-sufficient from the tourist's point of view. In winter she offers an attractive opportunity for leisure in the mountains; in the summer all her people flock to the seaside or to the lakes. All year round the innumerable

hikers' and ramblers' routes invite the enthusiasts of walking holidays, charming them in the springtime with all the shades of fresh green grasses, trees and shrubs, and all the colours of the flowers; or enticing them with the glowing hues of autumn.

Mountain ranges, for centuries the country's natural frontier, stretch from east to west right across Southern Poland. Only one route led through the mountains into Poland: through the pass called the Moravian Gate. It was along this route that in the times of the Roman Empire the famous Amber Way ran all the way to the Baltic coast, between the Sudety on the west and the Carpathian Mountains on the east. The highest Sudetan range comprises the extraordinarily picturesque Karkonosze. Air and water have carved them into intriguing shapes which endow these mountains with a special moonscape character.

The Carpathians stretch in a huge arch away into the Ukraine and Rumania and entail a variety of landscapes. The Rocky Tatras, aloof and inaccessible, tower over the entire countryside. The far more gently-sloping ranges of the Beskidy are beautiful especially in the autumn with their russet beech-woods. The wild Bieszczady with their *połonina* mountain pastures, little Eastern-rite churches, and ghost villages allure and inspire the imagination.

To the north beyond the line of the Sudety and Carpathians the land gradually drops, to form first a zone of picturesque uplands covered with a chessboard of small fields difficult to cultivate. Here and again weird and bewildering monadrocks loom up in the Cracovian and Częstochowa Jura, crested with the ruins of medieval castles, the inaccessible Eagle's Perches; in the region of Sandomierz loess ravines dissect the terrain. The final echo of Poland's mountain scenery are the Holy Cross Mountains (*Góry Świętokrzyskie*), old and low. Their highest ridge is spanned by the magnificent, lofty Pine Forest (*Puszcza Jodłowa*), which Stefan Żeromski described as 'sacred, belonging only to God'. On the mysterious bare rocks of *Święty Krzyż* (Holy Cross Mountain), a mighty concourse of boulders that look like the Creator's caprice, legends have always located the sabbaths where witches from the whole country were said to have congregated. Further north there are only the wide stretches of nostalgic lowland, cut across by the blue band of the Vistula, monarch of all Polish rivers, which widens out more and more into a lazy meander the nearer its ultimate destination. Here even life seems to move at a slower pace, less intensively than in the mountains, as if man accommodated his livelihood to the current of the river, and to the endless, monotonous landscapes of row upon row of bending willows. To the east of Mazovia, the territory of Podlassia (*Podlasie*) seems to strangers like a wilderness. It is spanned by the Forest of Białowieża (*Puszcza Białowieska*), one of Europe's last remaining stretches of primeval forest, a quite extraordinary reservation, a paradise for wild animals and nature-lovers. The wooden cottages, windmills and icons along the roadside, the picturesque Orthodox churches (here most of the local population is Orthodox), the virgin forests, the meadows along the River Bug and the marshlands on the banks of the Narew give landscapes as if specially set for the painter's easel and brush.

This scenery finds a rival in Masuria and Augustów, land of a thousand lakes. Maybe there aren't a thousand, but who would bother to count them all. Tiny tarns glistening in the midst of woodland, and huge lakes like Śniardwy, Mamry, Niegocin and Wigry comprise a complex system of waterways linked by a network of sluices and canals necessary for regulation, as the lakes are all at different levels. One of the human groups to have appreciated the charm of these wilds were the hermits of the Camaldolese Order, who always selected beautifully scenic settings for their abodes, to foster a life of contemplation. Here in a former Camaldolese hermitage on Lake Wigry Pope John Paul II spent a few hours of rest, recuperating his strength for the next stages of his 1999 Pontifical visit to Poland. Thanks to the network of canals joining the lakes, Masuria and the Lakeland of Augustów are a yachters' and kayakists' paradise. The region offers excellent tourist facilities, everything a water-sports enthusiast could wish for. That's why each year more and more rowers, kayakers, and anglers are coming here. Those who want just peace and quiet should choose the Pomeranian Lakes, or the amazing and unspoiled *Szwajcaria Kaszubska* (Cassubian 'Switzerland').

From there it's only a stone's throw to the Baltic: over five hundred kilometres of coastline, most of its gently undulating down to the seashore, with sandy beaches peppered by pieces of glistening amber washed ashore by the tide. Over the millennia the industrious waves have built up two picturesque sand-bars, the Vistulan (*Wiślana*) and the Hel Peninsula, both of which enclose tranquil bays. This part of the Baltic is quieter and less troublesome for sailing; its location is all the more favourable for being close to the estuary of the Vistula with its two major branches. For centuries the estuary has been guarded over by Gdańsk, city and port, window onto the world for the erstwhile Kingdom of Poland. But the sea means more than just commerce; it also offers marvellous recreation. This is to be had thanks to the warm sand along the beaches here, plentiful from the Rozewie Headland on the country's northernmost spit of land, right through to Międzyzdroje and Wolin Island in the delta of the Oder, Poland's second longest river. Between those two places a continuous battle is still being waged between land and sea. Precipitous snippets of coastline are being snatched away and submerged under the pressing waves, while elsewhere lakes like Gardno, Łebsko, or Jamno were in all likelihood cut off from the open sea at some time in the distant past.

All of Poland's landscapes, from mountains to seashore, were formed over the course of thousands of years. The towns and cities, villages, castles, and monasteries scattered over them also took a long time – centuries — to be built and acquire their present-day appearance, although they seem to have been created in one breath, as if in one final brushstroke. Without them the picture would be incomplete, without that polish of the finished work.

The sea in the
neighbourhood
of Rozewie,
the northernmost
part of Poland

Lake Wigry, with the silhouette of the former Camaldolese Hermitage. The Pope took his day of rest here during his 1999 visit to Poland

Podlassia. It will soon
be harvest-time...

'To those fields covered with the colours of many crops...'

A bend on the River Bug at Drohiczyn. View from the Castle Hill *(Góra Zamkowa)*, which towers over the countryside

Bison sanctuary in the
Forest of Białowieża

A woodland
thicket in the Vale
of the Biebrza

Vistulan mud-flats
near Kazimierz Dolny

29

Wąwóz Królowej Jadwigi, a loess gorge near Sandomierz

The Holy Cross
Mountains. The old
Benedictine Abbey
on *Święty Krzyż*
(Holy Cross Mountain)
stands in the middle
of the pine forest

View of Szczeliniec,
the highest peak
of the Table Mountains
(919 m.)

Autumn amid the
rocks of the Ojców
National Park

The white rocks of the
Valley of the Prądnik,
a typical landscape
in the Cracovian and
Częstochowa Jura

Harvest in the
fields around
Lake Rożnowskie

Panorama of the Tatras. In the right weather the summits of Poland's highest mountains may be visible even from Cracow, over 100 km away

Trzy Korony Mountain
in the Pieniny Range,
with the picturesque
Dunajec Gorge
at its foot

Panorama of the
Bieszczady Mountains
with a view onto the
Połonina Wetlińska
and Połonina Caryńska
mountain meadows

51

Symbols

Every nation and society has places, objects, events and figures in its history which have a symbolic meaning for it. Some are absolutely self-evident, others require explanation, but a knowledge of them is always necessary to locate one's co-ordinates in time and space.

One of the most patent symbols is the national emblem, for Poland the White Eagle with which the kings of Poland from the first Piastian monarchs to Stanisław August Ponia-towski (1763–1795) used as their device. But its appearance, with its ominous claws, changed over the centuries, subject to the tastes and styles of the princes, the times, and their political desiderata. This speci-men, one of the finest versions of the Polish Eagle, from the arms of Stephen Bathory (1576–1586), carrying that king's personal device, the Three Fangs, on its breast, was used in times which still witnessed the might of the Conjoined Common-weal of Poland and Lithuania. It goes back to Jagiellonian times, and it was in the closing period of the hereditary monarchy that the Polish Eagles were at their finest.

Symbolic figures: at the dawn of Polish history there are two such marking characters: Mieszko I and his son and heir, Boleslaus the Brave, founders of the sovereign Polish State. In 966 Mieszko made his realm part of Christendom, and Boleslaus turned it into an important European monarchy. Over 800 years after their deaths a mausoleum was erected in their honour. The mortal remains of father and son rest in the Byzantinesque splendour of the Golden Chapel in the Cathedral at Poznań, regional capital of Greater Poland *(Wielkopolska)*, cradle of Polish statehood (hence the name).

Symbolic places are often located on the map of a nation's awareness. Poland has at least two such places of worship: its principal Cathedral at Gniezno, and Wawel Cathedral. The former is connected with the country's most ancient history. Here, a thousand years ago, Boleslaus the Brave offered hospitality – and amazed his guests by its sumptuous pomp and ceremony – to the Empe-ror Otto III, a prince who dreamed of a united Europe. The event was marked by an act founding an archdiocese at Gniezno, confirming the young Polish Church's autonomy. The story of those turbulent times is told in the legend of St. Adalbert, depicted in the 12th-century cast bronze of the double door of Gniezno Cathedral. Its 18 panels present the life and martyrdom of this Bishop of Prague who set off on a mission to convert the tribes living along the north-eastern border of Poland. After his murder by the Prussians, King Boleslaus ransomed his body for its weight in gold and buried it in Gniezno Cathedral. A Czech bishop became a Polish saint, one of the national patrons, and also one of the mentors of the Christian community of Central Europe. Symbols often turn out to defy political borders and divisions; their power extends over and above political labelling and those who would reduce them to the role of local curiosities.

Wawel Cathedral is a treasury of symbols in itself: coronation church of the kings of Poland and royal bu-rial place, last resting place of the nation's most illustrious sons, a church charged with an immense meaning for the whole nation, al-though Cracow has not been Po-land's capital for around 400 years.

Places in the Polish cosmos have acquired symbolic qualities in numerous ways. Sometimes by the drama of history and the tragedy of many human destinies entrapped in the inevitability of the times. The fields of Grunwald, where in 1410 one of medieval Europe's biggest and last battles was fought between the Teutonic Knights and the victorious Polish and Lithuanian forces. Racławice, witness to the bravery of the Polish peasants who in 1794 marched (under Bartosz Głowacki) with their scythes in support of the regular troops under Tadeusz Kościuszko in a last-stand defence of Poland's independence against the Russians. Radzymin near Warsaw, site in 1920 of the 'Miracle on the Vistula' which was no miracle but a dearly paid for victory of the Polish army defending their capital, and also their newly recovered independence, against the Soviet forces. They are all symbolic of the glory and greatness of Polish arms. *Dulce et decorum est pro patria mori...*

But there are also monuments on Polish soil which stand as symbols to those to whom fate assigned a more difficult destiny. One is the Warsaw Uprising Monument, on one of those spots where for 63 days in the summer of 1944 Polish men and women endeavoured alone to challenge their enemy and their history; another is the Memorial of the Fallen Shipyard Workers which commemorates the tragic events of December 1970, when the Communist authorities issued the order to fire at the working class of Gdańsk.

Finally there are the very special places of suffering and humiliation, like Auschwitz, Europe's largest and most sombre charnel-house, where

the wind scattered the ashes of millions of Jews, Romany People, Poles and other nationals tortured to death and burned in the concentration camp crematoria; or the Memorial which calls to mind the places in the Siberian wasteland where millions of Polish citizens were deported to die. It is a good thing that no-one any longer denies the right to the those to whom this monument is dedicated to live on in the nation's memory.

There are also other special places which house the sanctuaries of the nation's faith, and the most prominent of these is Jasna Góra with its Pauline Monastery and the Holy Picture of the Black Madonna of Częstochowa. On this image of Our Lady, often referred to by Poles as the Queen of Poland, the nation's affection and awareness is singularly focused, making Jasna Góra rise up to the height of a conspicuously clear symbol.

Among all those battlefields, monuments to dedication and suffering, and the shrines, a special place is accorded to the achievements of the spirit, intellect and culture. They would not be there if it were not for Poland's Alma Mater, the Jagiellonian University of Cracow. It was founded in 1364 by Casimir the Great, the last monarch of the Piastian dynasty. But it has its growth and subsequent greatness to thank to the generous renewal foundation

made by St. Jadwiga and her husband King Vladislaus Jagiełło, the Royal Couple who initiated the new dynasty. The great astronomer Nicolaus Copernicus studied here in the late 15th century. Thanks to the learning he acquired here he ventured to challenge the world with his new heliocentric theory, 'stopping the Sun and moving the earth' and making a major contribution to scientific achievement.

Our brief and patently subjective journey through Poland's symbols concludes with two personalities which form as it were the framework to this photographic narrative: the Polish Pope who has guided the Roman Catholic Church for over two decades, and Lech Wałęsa, the man who for many symbolises the Polish transformations and road to liberty, retrieved in 1989.

There is no fixed canon of symbols; but there are symbols which do not change with the changes in people's preferences and ways of thinking. These are the ones that have been chosen here: people and places abiding in the history and awareness of the Polish nation, making up its identity. In his photographs Adam Bujak is our guide through the labyrinth of this treasure-house, wiping away the dust of history to enable the recalled images to shine in the full light of a language disused in everyday affairs but certainly far from extinct.

The Polish Eagle
with the arms of King
Stephen Báthory
(Three Fangs):
16th-century
escutcheon from
Włocławek
Cathedral

Mieszko I and
Boleslaus the Brave.
The Golden Chapel
of Poznań Cathedral
is the burial place of
Poland's first kings
and princes of the
Piast dynasty

Gniezno Cathedral, erected in the Gothic style in the 14th century, on the foundations of an earlier Romanesque structure; mementoes of the millennial history of the Archdiocese of Gniezno

56

The Double Door of Gniezno Cathedral, late 12th century, one of the most valued specimens of Romanesque art in Europe. Its 18 panels show the story of the life and martyrdom of St. Adalbert

Wawel Cathedral, Cracow; from the 14th century this Gothic cathedral was the coronation church and final resting place of the kings of Poland

Statue of Nicolaus
Copernicus, Toruń.
The heliocentric theory
put forward by the
Polish scientist
transformed our
image of the universe

The Collegium
Maius, the oldest,
15th-century, edifice
of the Jagiellonian
University of Cracow,
Poland's most ancient
university, and one of
the earliest universities
in Central Europe.
It was founded by
King Casimir the Great
in 1364

The Monastery of Jasna
Góra, Częstochowa,
founded in the 14th
century for the Pauline
Order, which was
brought to Poland from
Hungary. In 1655 the
fortified monastery
withstood the siege
during the Swedish
Invasion

The Chapel of Our Lady Queen of Poland at Jasna Góra. According to legend, the Icon of the Black Madonna, the object of special veneration among the Polish people, was painted by St. Luke on a cypress board from a table from the Virgin's house in Nazareth

63

The fields of Grunwald. Here on 15th July 1410 the last, and one of the biggest of all medieval battles was fought. The forces of Poland, Lithuanian, and Ruthenia, led by King Vladislaus Jagiełło and Prince Witold, vanquished the army of the Teutonic Knights who were assisted by knights from other parts of Europe

The mound at Racławice, a memorial to the 2,000 brave peasants who, under their leader Bartosz Głowacki, on 4th April 1794 came to the aid of the Polish forces under Tadeusz Kościuszko fighting to defend Poland's independence

The Polish soldiers'
grave at Radzymin.
Here on the outskirts
of Warsaw,
on 13th-15th August
1920, the Poles fought
and won a victory
against the Russian
Bolsheviks.

BRATNIA MOGIŁA
OHATERÓW POLEGŁYCH
RONIE OJCZYZNY w 1920 R.

WANA OFIARNOŚCIĄ PRACOWNIKÓW

BANKV POLSKIEGO w WARSZAWIE

To those who fell or were murdered in the East: this Monument is a tribute to all the Polish citizens, of many religions and national and ethnic groups, who were deported to Soviet Russia, beyond the Ural, Siberia, or to Kazakhstan and other distant lands, and who suffered oppression and died there

Auschwitz, the Nazi death camp. The inscription over the gate reads *Arbeit macht frei* (Work makes you free), but this was not a place for either work or freedom. Here and in the neighbouring camp of Birkenau millions – Jews, Romany People, citizens of Poland and virtually of all the occupied countries of Europe – were killed

69

Monument of the Warsaw Uprising, which broke out on 1st August 1944 and continued for sixty-three days – watched from the other bank of the Vistula by the Red Army, which stood idly by while Warsaw was bleeding to death

Pope John Paul II and
President Lech Wałęsa
two great figures,
symbols of modern
Poland

72

Gdańsk, Shipyard Workers' Memorial. In December 1970 the shipyard workers of Gdańsk came out on strike. They died from bullets shot by Polish soldiers; Polish generals issued the order to fire

Strongholds

Castles have always given the feeling of security; they were symbols of strength, power, and authority. From the walls of his castle the lord could look down onto his lands; in it he would feel invulnerable; from it he would rule his domain. Times have changes; the wheel of history has turned; the age of the castles has long since passed. Once seats of powerful families, residences of princes, strongholds defending a country's frontiers, today they have turned into tourist attractions for their rich histories and picturesque settings. Some are nothing more than ruins, tell-tale signs of a turbulent history and fascinating for their mysterious beauty; others have become magnificent stately homes, having lost their now redundant defence walls and towers. The castles of Poland are a testimony to the might and affluence of that country and its dignitaries; a souvenir of its unique history at the crossroads of many cultures but in the very heart of Europe; a vestige of its countless wars inscribed into the stones, but also evidence of the wealth and love of beautiful architecture that marked many a proprietor and builder of these keeps.

Of the oldest medieval castles, Gothic fortresses guarding the Piastian realm, mostly only ruins are left; their walls could not withstand the new developments in besieging, and they would fall in the course of subsequent wars or simply to the effects of time. Sinking more and more into their natural surroundings, the skeletons of these ancient strongholds have now more or less coalesced with the local scenery and allure the 20th-century observer with their romantic charm, reminding him of bygone ages and inspiring his imagination with the stories of the ghosts that haunt them. There is no dearth of such places in Poland. It is enough to think of the old Eagles' Nests – a fully justified name for a line of ancient keeps on the ridge of the Cracovian and Częstochowa Jura, or the ruins like the castle at Zagórze Śląskie, once the seat of the dukes of Silesia.

Ruins give only an idea of the erstwhile size and strength of the stronghold. They exact admiration for the medieval art of architecture which permitted the construction of such extraordinary edifices that their ruins are so fascinating even today.

Not all the medieval castles fell into ruin, of course, through the devastation wreaked by man or nature. On the northern edges of modern Poland there are fortresses which recall a power once inimical to the Polish state – the Teutonic Order. The mightiest of them, Malbork, is Europe's largest extant medieval stronghold in brickwork, fascinating visitors by its huge size, the grandeur of its architecture, and the boldness of its construction scheme: a residence truly worthy of the Grand Master of the Teutonic Order, who from 1309 ruled his principality from here. Not very far away, in Lidzbark Warmiński, there is the 14th-century castle of the bishops of Varmia, one of the most valuable specimens of defence architecture in Poland. The appearance of castles changed with the changes in military and siege-laying techniques. At the peak of the Renaissance thanks to Poland's power castles could be built or converted in such a way as to combine a sense of security with sophisticated elegance to please both their masters and guests. The mightiest strongholds guarded the country's eastern marchlands, often referred to as the antemurale Christianitiatis – the bulwark of Christendom; but the centrally located ones, in areas where there was no imminent threat, would be constructed just as conscientiously. The strength of their walls served as a material token of the proprietor's wealth and status. Residences were erected rivalling Italian counterparts, for they were built by Italian masters like Bartolommeo Berrecci and Santi Gucci, designers respectively of Wawel Castle and Baranów Castle near Sandomierz.

Castle conversions were carried out by monarchs – Sigismundus the Old and his Italian consort Bona Sforza, and their son, last of the Jagiellons, who endowed Wawel Castle with an absolutely new character. But conversions or building schemes were also accomplished by magnates, sometimes more opulent than many a prince, no wonder then that the castles at Wiśnicz, Pieskowa Skała, and Krasiczyn are on a par with royal residences, or even surpass them.

New styles would be combined with existing components, giving rise to interesting amalgamations, such as the one at Lublin, where a Renaissance architecture surrounds a medieval defence keep with a Gothic chapel decorated with unique late 14th-century frescoes. New constructions would be erected in accordance with the Italian palazzo in fortezza fashion, combining comfort and elegance with the defence features of the castle's location.

The 17th and 18th centuries and their interminable wars which rolled disastrously over Poland brought destruction to many of the castles, both those still being used for defence purposes and those which had become more of a country residence than a military stronghold. Krzysztof Ossolinski, master of Krzyżtopór Castle in Ujazd, one of the most magnificent specimens of fortification construction in Poland, did not enjoy his exceptional residence for long. He died a year after it was finished, and perhaps it was just as well that he did not live to see the utter destruction 20 years later, during the Swedish invasion, of architect Lorenzo Senes' splendid creation, which had as many windows as there are days in the year, as many rooms as there are weeks, as many halls as there are months, and as many towers as there are seasons. The next centuries were marked by the Baroque residences, with their fondness for vales and gardens. The vogue for castles adaptations in various styles would return in the 19th century, along with the penchant for follies reminiscent of medieval Gothic and other bygone fashions in building. One of the finest examples of such trends is Kórnik Castle, once a Renaissance residence belonging to the Górka family, but converted in a Neo-Gothic style in the early 19th century by Tytus Działyński, its proprietor at the time. The end result was a typically Romantic structure modelled on the medieval castles and Late English Gothic. Działyński saw the residence he had created as 'premises to house the national monuments'. Like the Czartoryski and Działyński residences, Gołuchów Castle, which was being rebuilt in the same period in a French Renaissance style not very typical for Poland, was envisaged as a museum. Castles, once seats of ancient families, thus became secure quarters not just for their lords, but also for the national heritage of art and culture.

The Royal Castle on Wawel Hill, Cracow, for centuries the main residence of the kings and princes of Poland. It was turned in to a Renaissance structure in the 16th century by King Sigismundus the Old and his Italian consort, Bona Sforza

The throne wall in the Hall of Senators at Wawel Castle, decorated by one of the arrases from the magnificent 16th-century collection of King Sigismundus Augustus. This arras shows a Biblical scene the Deluge

Part of the Renaissance arcade around the courtyard of Baranów Castle. It was probably designed by the Italian architect Santi Gucci, who spent many years working in Poland and made his finest creations here

The Renaissance edifice of Baranów Castle near Sandomierz was built for Rafał Leszczyński and his son the Lord Voivode Andrzej Leszczyński, a great patron of the arts and an adherent of the Reformation

Łańcut Castle,
residence of Polish
aristocracy. In the 18th
and 19th centuries its
bastion fortifications
were demolished
and the fortress was
transformed into a
splendid *palazzo*
surrounded by an
extensive park – as
befitted the wealth of
the Lubomirski and
Potocki families

The dormeuse, travelling carriage, and luggage cab, some of the many fascinating vehicles in the coach-house at Łańcut Castle

Wiśnicz Castle, in a mixed Gothic/Renaissance style, was owned by the aristocratic families of Kmita and Lubomirski. Over the centuries it was developed and fortified in accordance with the requirements of European military engineering, but its aesthetics were in the local, somewhat eastern spirit

87

The bastioned structure of Krasiczyn Castle was erected at the turn of the 16th and 17th centuries by Jakub and Stanisław Krasicki. Its four corner bastions, the Divine, Pontifical, Royal, and Noble Bastions, reflect the four pillars of cosmic order

The Renaissance-style
Royal Castle at Lublin,
with a huge keep
which survives from
the previous structure
on the site, an early
medieval stronghold

Ceiling of the chapel in Lublin Castle, with unique Old Ruthenian wall paintings (turn of the 14th and 15th centuries)

Bastioned structure
of Rzeszów Castle,
mid-17th century,
erected by Jerzy
Lubomirski, Lord Grand
Marshal of the Realm

Gołuchów Castle, a Renaissance structure which belonged to the aristocratic family of Leszczyński, of Greater Poland. In the 19th century it was converted in a French style by Izabela Działyńska, to house a rich art collection

Pieskowa Skała Castle, 14th century. It received its 16th-century Renaissance form and nickname of 'the Little Wawel' thanks to Stanisław Szafraniec, one of the principal figures in public life at the time

Kórnik Castle, once
a Renaissance structur
In the 19th century
Tytus Działyński
commissioned the
well-known Berlin
architect, Karl Friedric
Schinkel, to carry
out a Neo-Gothic
conversion on it

The Mauretanian Room in Kórnik Castle. Kórnik houses a magnificent art collection and an extremely rich collection of early printed works, known as the Kórnik Library

Castle of the Dukes of Pomerania, Szczecin. This medieval stronghold was converted in the 16th century in an Italian Renaissance style, probably by Italian architects

Malbork Castle, headquarters of the Grand Master of the Teutonic Knights, erected in the early 14th century and subsequently developed and modernised. Europe's largest Gothic fortress

Lidzbark Castle,
14th century, residence
of the bishops of
Varmia. The last
incumbent prelate
was Ignacy Krasicki,
a distinguished
Enlightenment poet

Ruins of Grodno Castle at Zagórze in Silesia (14th century), once held by the local duke

Niedzica Castle, a medieval structure which belonged to a succession of noble families. At the turn of the 16th and 17th centuries, when in the hands of the Horwath family of Hungary, it was converted and reinforced with corner-bastions

Residences

The house which stood at the centre of a country estate was as it were its heart, a focus for all the virtues and values. Styles, periods, customs, and proprietors' wealth have made some mansions and residences astonish us with their elegance and splendour, and others, on the contrary – charm us with their modesty and simplicity. There is no dearth in Poland of examples of the idiosyncratic affection lavished on the family home – whether palace, mansion or the Polish-styled *dwór* or *dworek*, from the royal palace at Wilanów, through the lordly residences such as Łańcut, to the humble gentleman's dwór at Ożarów.

The palatial residences and country *dwory*, which answered the needs of the times, took the place of the castles. Already in the mid-17th century the author of 'a short treatise on the science of building *dwory* and palaces according to the Polish clime and custom' wrote that country mansions were better suited *ad usum* of the Polish policy than compacted castles, for the reason that a 'longitudinal mansion with extensive grounds rather than an enclosed courtyard like a castle, and with other buildings next to it, could be more advantageous and less subject to the foul air.' His advice was that it was better to build a single, long mansion than to squeeze everything into a castle. Moreover, after the devastating wars of the 17th century, in many cases it was absolutely necessary to build a new residence. The needs and expectations of the increasingly wealthier noble families had changed. Their social status called for suitable expression. The stately home, which displayed its opulence to the outside world already along the tree-lined drive leading through its grounds up to an ornate façade and heralding the magnificence of its interior, was better accommodated to the tastes and attitudes of the new age; while the customs of the Sarmatian equestrian society made their influence felt on the shape and form of these houses. Another significant factor was the proprietors' fondness for the country and their rural lifestyle, and attempts were made to incorporate a token of this even in and around their town houses. What distinguished Polish residential architecture was on the one hand the persistence of defence structures, original or ornamental, and on the other the adaptive harmonising of the edifice into the setting of its landscape and grounds. This may be observed both in the exquisite Royal Palace of Wilanów, at Puławy, residence of the Czartoryski family, and in the *dwór* at Glanów on the outskirts of Cracow. Accentuating defence structures gave a specific mode for the emphasis of opulence. In the more modest homes this role was played by alcoves flanking the façades, as may bee seen in the construction of the wooden *dwór* at Ożarów, one of the finest specimens of the old Polish art of building. Thus residences would be raised in accordance with one of two recipes: the first alluded to the Italian villa style, and the second evolved out of the native tradition of residential architecture situated on a rectangular plan. There would be designed by the best architects from Italy, France, the Low Countries or Germany. The less well-off landed gentry followed the styles of the nobility's mansions, and in this way by the late 18th century the classic model of the Polish *dwór* had developed, with a projection instead of the old alcove and a representational portico, a picturesque mansard roof and dormer windows. Splendid examples of the Polish *dwór* may be observed at Złoty Potok, next to the country mansion, and also at Nagłowice and Czarnolas, where the memories and mementoes of the 16th-century poets, Mikołaj Rej and

Jan Kochanowski, their respective masters, are still cherished. The Polish gentleman's *dwór* rose to a symbolic position, entrenched even more profoundly by the dramatic events under the Partitions and the loss of national independence, when it was precisely in these family homes that the ideas behind the uprisings against the partitioning powers were born, while later their proprietors paid for the love of freedom and their country with deportation and confiscation of their property. In public awareness the *dwór* came to be not only an inseparable part of the countryside, but above all the hub of all that was crucial to the Polish gentlefolk's tradition. This feeling was intensified even more by the association of many of these country homes with the outstanding personalities of Polish history – Śmiełów, where Adam Mickiewicz stayed; Żelazowa Wola, Chopin's birthplace.

On the other hand the appeal of the royal and magnates' palaces is in the magnificence of their interior decoration, and in the richness and beauty of the works of art and architecture they contain. Those which have survived the turmoil of war offer a reminiscence of the splendour of their masters' lives. The Łazienki Palace at Warsaw, the Branicki Palace at Białystok, often referred to as the Versailles of Podlassia, the Hochenberg residence at Pszczyna, and the

Czartoryskis' Palace at Puławy – these are just some of the examples from a long list of exquisite residences of a European standard of grandeur and luxury.

The romantic tendency to create a Polish gentry and equestrian mythology around the past, and the general nostalgia for former glory gave rise in the 19th century to a fashion for purely decorative, mock defensive architectural forms. This was the style of the *dworek* at Oblęgorek which the nation donated in gratitude to the novelist Henryk Sienkiewicz; and of the country house at Olszanica, at the feet of the Bieszczady Mountains. Their corner turrets, bay windows, fanciful attics and carved ornamentations clashed with the Neo-Classical concepts of harmony and symmetry, but it was thanks to these details that these homes have their stunning appeal and charm.

In spite of the architectural changes, the Sarmatian-styled model of the Polish country house proved extremely enduring, as a place where the memory of the Poland of old is still fresh, the hearth-side of patriotism and the treasury of tradition. That is why, after so many years of enthralment, the owner of one of these houses had the following motto carved into the façade of his property, 'I am the Polish dwór, I fight valiantly and I faithfully defend.' It was these homes of the Polish

country gentlemen that kept their faith and preserved the cosmos of the ancient virtues for future generations, those which again are free.

Wilanów Palace, a Baroque residence on the outskirts of Warsaw owned by King John III Sobieski, and later to the aristocratic families of Potocki and Branicki

Łazienki Palace, and the Palace on the Lake, Poland's most beautiful Early Classical palace and grounds, built by Stanisław August Poniatowski, last King of Poland

Baroque residence of
the Branicki family at
Białystok, known as the
Versailles of Podlassia,
one of the largest
palace and park
arrangements in Poland

The Palace of the
Bishops of Cracow
was commissioned
in Kielce in the early
17th century by
Bishop Jakub Zadzik.
This Early Baroque
residence has
preserved an
exceptional stylistic
uniformity

Residence of the Silesian family of the Dukes of Pszczyna and Hochberg in Pszczyna, a Baroque edifice converted in the 19th century and set in a magnificent landscape park

Puławy Palace. The most glorious period in the history of this Baroque structure is associated with Prince Adam Czartoryski and his wife Izabela, prominent patrons of Polish culture at the turn of the 18th and 19th centuries

Delightful wooden hunting lodge at Antonin, early 19th century, designed by Karl Friedrich Schinke Prince Antoni Radziwi hosted Frédéric Chop here.

Romantic early
19th-century residence
at Olszanica at the
feet of the Bieszczady
Mountains

123

Wooden *dwór* at Janowiec on the Vistula, in the park around the ruins of a Renaissance castle. The wooden construction was moved here from the village of Moniaki in the region of Lublin

18th-century Neo-Classical *dwór* at Glanów, Lesser Poland, famous for the heroic defence it put up during the January Uprising of 1863

This wooden alcoved *dwór* at Ożarów near Wieluń was built in 1757. Its two alcoves at the corners of the front wall go back to the tradition of the old fortified constructions

This Neo-Classical *dwór*, set in a park at Czarnolas near Radom, does not remember the times of the most famous master of this property, the principal Polish Renaissance poet Jan Kochanowski, since its present form was not built until the mid 19th century

The Neo-Classical
dwór at Nagłowice
(turn of the 18th and
19th centuries) was
erected on the site
of the residence once
owned by Mikołaj Rej,
an outstanding
Renaissance poet
and promoter of the
Reformation

The Neo-Classical
country house at
Śmiełów is one
of the most elegant
residences in Greater
Poland. In 1831
Adam Mickiewicz
stayed here, during
an attempt to reach
combatants fighting in
the November Uprising

133

The Neo-Classical
residence in Złoty Po
once belonged to
Zygmunt Krasiński,
an eminent Polish
Romantic poet

This country house at Oblęgorek, built in an eclectic style in the late 19th century, was presented to the novelist Henryk Sienkiewicz by the nation

135

The *dworek* at Żelazowa Wola, Mazovia, birthplace and childhood home of Frédéric Chopin

Cities

The history of the oldest Polish towns and cities is longer than the history of the Polish state, and their origins go back to the fortified keeps or boroughs situated at strategic locations such as hilltops, fords, mountain passages into distant lands – all convenient and easily safe-guarded sites. Self-sufficient in status, they were rather like the *poleis* of Antiquity, with an inner centre of government and an accretion of foreboroughs.

We do not know which of the municipalities on Polish soil is the oldest. However, we do know which have the most ancient records. Kalisz was mentioned by the Alexandrian geographer Claudius Ptolemy, who lived in the 2nd century A.D. He entered the town *Calisia* on a map in his *Geography*. Later archaeologists confirmed his situation and were able to identify Calisia with Kalisz, a medium-sized munici-pality in today's Poland.

Calisia developed thanks to the Roman ladies' love of amber. The place was at a convenient spot on the road that led from Rome to the Baltic, where the tide continually washes ashore these glittering golden stones. Kalisz found itself between the source of the merchandise and the market for it, at the right place, ideal for the establishment of a town, the size, power and status of which would depend on the volume and growth of trade. The history of many of Poland's cities is frequently tanta-mount to the history of the trading routes through them – a record of the traffic of goods and services. In the early Middle Ages the continuation of the old towns, and the establishment of new ones, came to depend on the will of the king or prince and on his country's prosperity. The towns of Lower Silesia, such as Paczków, sometimes referred to as the Polish Carca-ssonne (and for good reason, too), thrived under the Piast dynasty; so did the towns of Lesser Poland after the capital was moved to Cracow. King Casimir the Great, who reigned in the 14th century, is regarded as the greatest benefactor of Poland's towns. He founded many new ones; and a couple of them, such as Kazimierza Wielka and Kazimierz (now a quarter of Cracow) honour him in their very names. He put new defence walls round the existing towns; and he followed a wise set of policies,

creating excellent conditions for the advancement of the urban communi-ties.

In later times many towns were established as private foundations; the most powerful lords whose colossal wealth permitted enterprises on such a scale granted municipal charters. One of the most prominent of the privately founded towns was Zamość, set up in 1580 at the behest of one individual, Jan Zamoyski, Lord Chancellor of the Realm. To accomplish his undertaking Zamoyski employed the services of numerous foreigners, including the Italian Bernardo Morando, who designed the architectural layout for the entire town, with the latest scheme for bastion fortifications on a pentago-nal plan. Morando also designed many of the individual town houses. Thanks to this Zamość was given an exceptionally uniform arrangement. It is sometimes called the Padua of the North, both on account of its architectural elegance, and also because of its erstwhile college, the Akademia Zamojska. The town was indeed the feather in Zamoyski's cap, far more beautiful than the Leszczyńskis' Leszno in Greater Poland, the Tarnowskis' and Ostrogskis' Tarnów in Lesser Poland, or the Szydłowieckis' Szydłowiec. Most of these municipalities were grand for as long as their founders remained in office, but vestiges of their former splendour have been preserved in the historic heirlooms which may still be observed in these towns.

There are many towns in Poland which had their moments of glory and later, along with changing times and tides of fortune, faded away into the ordinary and unexceptional. The houses lining their marketplaces, the dignified town halls, the elegant churches, and the mighty walls in many of these, now provincial places, astound visitors and induce reflection on the whims of fortune. Gniezno is much smaller than Poznań, but it was Gniezno that hosted the Emperor Otto III and witnessed the birth of a new order in this part of Europe. Stary Sącz was once the first borough just over the border with Hungary where kings and foreign dignitaries on their way to the capital in Cracow would stop and be given a welcome. Biecz, Jarosław, and Przemyśl grew out of the trade with the Orient, thanks to the auspicious conditions for Ukrainian cereals and cattle, and eastern luxuries imported from the Ottoman Empire, the Crimea or Persia via the Black Sea ports. Kazimierz Dolny, one of the most charming of Poland's towns, owed its livelihood to the Vistula, the waterway down which goods such as wheat and timber would be transported in barges to Gdańsk, and from there out to the rest of Europe. Today the huge granaries

on the riverbank and the magnificent houses in the market place, once homes of the town's wealthy merchants, remind visitors of this fact. The towns of Mazovia, such as Łomża, Pułtusk and Ciechanów, sprang up in outcome of the fact that the Jagiellons, the Lithuanian dynasty on the Polish throne, made frequent progresses – both because of royal duties and homesickness – between Wilno and Cracow. It was a similar story with Lublin, which today holds a rather eastern position but was once almost centrally located in the conjoined state of the Kingdom of Poland and Grand Duchy of Lithuania, an excellent venue for the elected deputies of all of its scattered territories to convene, and the place where they ratified the Act of Union of 1569.

Today's capital, Warsaw, owes its modern status to an analogous political and geographical situation. In the 20th century the name of this city became synonymous with indomitable heroism, and then with the virtually superhuman effort made by its inhabitants raising it up anew out of the ruins of the Second World War.

There are also cities which have always been grand and aglow with the beauty of their municipal heritage. There is the port and trading city of Gdańsk, which has survived hard times and which today is once

again resplendent with its sumptuous town houses and its bold architecture. There is Poznań, cradle of Poland's statehood, a city which valiantly resisted Germanisation under the Partitions, and which today is the venue for international trade fairs attracting global business attention. Finally there is royal Cracow with its extraordinary *genius loci*, a city which has always been splendid, although in the past four centuries it has not exercised the role of state capital. It's no wonder Cracow attracts crowds of visitors from all over the world, who come to experience that rare atmosphere and admire Europe's biggest medieval market place. Poland has its historic cities, towns remarkable for their beauty, and towns which have changed with the times, trends, and economic ups and downs, focal points for its public life. From a tower on Wawel Cathedral, the one which houses the Sigismundian Bell and affords the best panorama view onto Cracow, you can observe all the different aspects of the life of this city, built so industriously by generations. The remarks of Ernst Jünger on the life of cities may be recalled here, 'Mother-of-pearl is formed by the arduous accumulation of layers, but that is not what makes it so valuable.' Poland has no dearth of such pearls.

Panorama of Gniezno, one of Poland's oldest towns, with the 14th-century Cathedral towering over it. In 1000 A.D. Gniezno offered hospitality to the Emperor Otto III.

141

Panorama of the Royal City of Cracow, a capital of Poland. The helms of Wawel Cathedral glisten in the background

Panorama of Warsaw's Old Town, with the characteristic outline of St. John's Cathedral. To humiliate the Polish nation, the Nazi occupying powers razed Warsaw to the ground, but after the War the Poles rebuilt their capital

The port area of Gdańsk, once window on the world for Poland-Lithuania. Gdańsk has its excellent location on the mouth of the Vistula to thank for its prosperity

Artus' Court, Gdańsk
(late 15th century),
old headquarters
of the merchant guild
a sign of the wealth
and power of this
Baltic port

148

The small town of
Gołuchów, one of
the many places which
owed its existence to
efficient management
of a local landlord

Lublin, the largest city in eastern Poland. It developed and acquired political significance thanks to an auspicious location, once in the very centre of the Commonwealth of the Conjoined Nations of Poland and Lithuania

The Old Town of Wrocław with the characteristic outline of its medieval town hall, which was built in the late 13th century, but not given its present-day shape until a 15th-century redevelopment

The town hall of Zamość, a municipality founded in 1580 by the Lord Chancellor Jan Zamoyski. Zamość is often referred to as the Padua of the North on account of its uniform Renaissance layout, designed by Bernardo Morando

Panorama of Przemyśl, which lies on either bank of the River San, near Poland's eastern border. A heterogeneous city, with a mixture of ethnic and national groups, cultures, and religions

155

Kazimierz Dolny on the Vistula. One of the most delightful small towns in Poland, situated on a cliff overlooking the Vistula. It thrived economically thanks to the river, once the trunk route for commerce

The medieval walls of Paczków. This little town in Silesia, with nineteen bastions and three gates, is sometimes called the Polish Carcassonne

The marketplace of Poznań, regional capital of Greater Poland. Its Renaissance town houses and magnificent guildhall testify to its erstwhile grandeur. Today Poznań is the venue for the international trade fair

Sandomierz on
the Vistula:
marketplace and
Renaissance town hall.
Picturesquely set on
a cliff overhanging the
Vistula, Sandomierz
is one of the prettiest
towns in Poland

Renaissance town hall in Tarnów, This municipality, owned by the Tarnowski and Ostrogski families, thrived thanks to its position on the east-west trading route

The extant part
of the municipal walls
of the small cathedral
town of Frombork,
where Copernicus
spent his last years
and is buried in the
Gothic Cathedral

An extraordinary, spectacular row of granaries lining the Vistula escarpment at Grudziądz. This town was a river port on the lower course of the Vistula and prospered thanks to the trade in wheat, which would be sent on from here to Gdańsk

Folklore

There is no one Polish folk culture. A variety of forms, models, and motifs have developed in accordance with their natural conditions and to a certain extent in isolation with respect to the neighbouring lands, not to mention remoter countries. Rivers and marshes, forests still uncleared, and later the frontiers of the three partitional zones comprised rarely negotiated barriers, partly for fear, partly for want of natural need. These borders were gradually obliterated, but the different patters created within them have remained. That is why today we have several distinctly different cultural regions, each unique, colourful, and full of inspiration.

One of the particularly interesting cultural enclaves is the Podhale mountain region at the feet of the Tatras, a most abundant treasury of folk motifs. Its assets were the earliest to be recognised, when convalescents started coming here,

in the late 19th century, for the crystal-clear mountain air. Since they included artists, who were able to appreciate more than the climatic advantages, Podhalanian art soon made its way into the exclusive drawing-rooms. On the basis of the local building models for cottages, mansard and shingled roofs with carved decorations on the eaves, doorposts and window casements, Stanisław Witkiewicz created a style of his own which he called the Zakopane Style, which was taken up in the private residential building crafts all over the country. A school for the arts and crafts was set up in Cracow in the early 20th century to train craftsmen and artists for design and crafts. It educated designers of furniture, textiles, and ceramics, all modelled on Podhalanian motifs. The Podhalanian traditional pictures painted on glass migrated to the cities, too. So did the local music, which proved a source of inspiration for renowned composers such as Karol Szymanowski.

Other regions, albeit just as colourful, weren't lucky enough to have such influential mentors. The painted cottages of Zalipie in the Powiśle region near Tarnów, never transcended the borders of that village and remained a local speciality. The womenfolk of Zalipie, who each year paint the walls, ceilings, stoves and fenders, utensils, wells, and even the dog-kennels of their homesteads with floral patterns, are still the exclusive experts

in this particular folk craft, and can only vie with each other. This they do, outdoing one another in designing ingenious flower and plant compositions, discovering any still unpainted surfaces in their cottages, and in the perfection of their lines and colour-schemes. They achieve amazing effects.

The Łowicz region, in Central Poland, has become famous for the woven and extremely colourful kirtles and aprons worn by the local women. The full costume sparkles with a riot of colours in the striped skirts, aprons, embroidered blouses and bodices, and beads. These villages were obviously well-off, and located in a good place for growth. It's not far from here to the Mazovian fields with their roadside weeping willows around Żelazowa Wola, where Chopin was born and as a child listened to the folk music from the local villages. The folk music motifs sank deep into his memory, and he would retrieve them in his famous mazurkas, polonaises, and nostalgic nocturnes.

Equally fascinating regions with a rich folk tradition are to be found in Kurpie, Podlassia, Silesia, Cassubia, and many other parts of Poland. Happily their culture has not disappeared in the confrontation with civilisation from the higher social echelons, as might have been feared inevitable. Museums of folk culture have preserved all the finest achievements of the small man's arts, crafts, and livelihood. In the Kurpie museum at Nowogród on the River Narew, in the Mazovian museum at Sierpc, at Kluki in Pomerania, Olsztynek in Masuria, Chorzów and Opole in Silesia, Tokarnia near Kielce, Sanok and Nowy Sącz in the Beskidy Mountains, Zubrzyca Górna in Oravia, and in many more places up and down Poland, you can look into the open-air folk museums to see and admire this great store of local culture. Only the Podhale still does not have an open-air museum of its own, but of course the whole of the Podhalanian region is one gigantic open-air exhibition in itself.

Rites and events testifying to non-material culture have proved even more enduring. Although the Polish countryside is rapidly being transformed, although the old cottages have been moved to the open-air museums, the ancient rural traditions and rites have survived and are performed with the regularity of the changing seasons and church festivals in the liturgical calendar, adding colour to the country way of life. The combination of the ancient pagan belief in the need to obtain the favour of the personified powers of nature, and of the Christian doctrine of God's assistance to man, which may be granted through the intercession of the Saints, and above all through the Virgin Mary, has given rise to an extremely rich and varied set of folk practices and customs accompanying the Christian (Roman and Uniate Catholic, and Orthodox) feasts and holy days. Alongside these there are also the Muslim folk rituals kept alive by the Polish Tartars. Thus at Christmastide cottages are decorated with colourful garlands hung up at the ceiling, and groups of carol-singers specially dressed up and carrying a Christmas crib, a revolving star on a long pole and an animal figure called a *turoń* wander about the villages. Eastern-rite Christians (Orthodox and Uniate) commemorate Jesus' baptism in the Jordan at the nearest riverside, where they are cleansed by the water. On Palm Sunday, to mark Jesus' triumphal entry into Jerusalem, there is a special service for the blessing of palms, which in many villages take on the form of huge sheaves of multi-coloured grasses, bulrushes, flowers and herbs. On average they measure about 6 metres, but the biggest, made by the womenfolk of the villages around Cracow and in the Kurpie, go up to 26 metres. They rival each other over whose 'palm' will be biggest and with the most original design. After having the palms blessed in church, they carry them out into the fields, to obtain the favour of Nature for their crops. At Kalwaria Zebrzydowska in Holy Week thousands of pilgrims come to attend the local Mysteries of the Passion, which commemorate the passion and death of Jesus.

A rich heritage of rites and customs is not the exclusive speciality of the country areas, although there it is assisted by the natural rhythm of the seasons and climate. The cities also have their festivals, often going back to the Middle Ages. The Cracovian Christmas cribs, which are presented every year in the Main Market Square on the first Thursday of December, are more reminiscent of the stately Cracovian ecclesiastical architecture than of the roughness of a real stable. The Christmas fare to be had from the booths set up for the occasion around the original Cloth Hall has become a favourite Cracovian form of Christmas shopping. But Cracow and the other cities are at their most festive in June, when they celebrate the Corpus Christi procession in the streets, with flower girls dropping petals before the priest carrying the monstrance with the Holy Sacrament. In Cracow this is followed, on the octave of the feast, by the gallivanting escapades of the Lajkonik Hobby-Horse. In summer Gdańsk invites visitors to its Dominican fair (early August); Poznań has its Malta Lake; and the mining towns of Silesia celebrate the feast of St. Barbara, patron saint of miners (4th December). Throughout the twelve months of the year in Poland tradition meets modernity, and the local folk customs make their presence felt in our national culture.

A roadside chapel, decorated with flowers and branches, of Jesus of Nazareth, at Kalwaria Zebrzydowska, a famous place of pilgrimage in southern Poland

Fisherman's cottage
near Kazimierz Dolny
on the Vistula

Open-air folklore
museum at Olsztynek:
a 19th-century
arcaded inn, from the
village of Burdajny in
the Powiśle region

173

Palm Sunday at Tokarnia. The local people make some of the largest Easter palms in Poland; some are over 20 m in height

175

A basket of Easter eggs decorated with patterns characteristic for Zalipie. Hand-painted Easter eggs, the pride of the local womenfolk, are taken to church on Holy Saturday in a basket with other foods for the traditional Easter blessing

The traditional method of tobacco leaf-drying under the cottage eaves in the region of Tomaszów Lubelski, a very fertile area

One of the innumerable roadside shrines or termini which would be put up at crossroads, or on the borders of villages and fields

179

Mallows growing in
a cottage garden
at Liw in Mazovia.
In Poland these slender
flowers are a must for
country gardens

A country cottage from the neighbourhood of Łęczyca, central Poland

182

Interior of a Zalipie cottage, with floral decorations. The women of Zalipie paint flower motifs on all the surfaces they have available – walls, stoves and fenders, furniture, and kitchen utensils, plates, crockery and tableware

A woman from a Lesser Polish village on August 15th, the feast of Our Lady of the Herbs; in accordance with the ancient custom, she brings a bunch of flowers and herbs to church for the traditional blessing

A young Łowicz girl in
her traditional costume:
a flowery bonnet,
a blouse embroidered
in a floral pattern,
and a typical striped,
gathered skirt

187

Singing Gypsy girls
in a caravan,
attending an annual
folk rally organised by
the regional museum
of Tarnów, which gets
a rich contribution
from the Polish
Romany People

Original cottage-shaped beehives in the village of Grabonóg, Greater Poland

19th-century
Christmas crib from
Wambierzyce,
Lower Silesia, with a
clockwork mechanism
moving the figures
to present New
Testament scenes

The real towers of
St. Mary's of Cracow
and as shown in the
Cracovian Christmas
cribs. These colourful
cribs come in various
sizes, but they always
carry motifs from
Cracow's architecture.
They are displayed
around the Mickiewicz
Monument on the first
Thursday in December.

The famous Lajkonik Hobby-Horse. Every year on the octave of Corpus Christi the Lajkonik and his retinue set out from the courtyard of the Premonstratensian Convent in Zwierzyniec for the Main Market Square

Cracow's Main
Market Square,
the biggest medieval
marketplace in Europe,
full of Christmas stalls

Garlands made for
the *dożynki* harvest
festival, a symbol of
a successful harvest

199

Rydlówka House in the former village of Bronowice (now a district of Cracow). In 1900 the wedding of the Cracovian poet Lucjan Rydel with Jadwiga Mikołajczykówna, daughter of a Bronowice farmer, was held here, and later immortalised in Stanisław Wyspiański's play *Wesele* (The Wedding)

Sabałowe bajanie, a folk festival of story-telling in the Podhalanian village of Bukowina Tatrzańska

The pipes helped to
make sheep-grazing
on the mountain
meadows more
enjoyable

Churches

In 966 Mieszko of the dynasty of Piast, Prince of Poland, wedded Dobrawa, a Czech Princess, and was baptised by Czech ecclesiasts. That moment is regarded as the beginning of Christianity on the territories under Piastian rule. Mieszko's son, Boleslaus, later called the Brave, continued his parents' work of bringing his people into the Christian fold and European civilisation. In the course of the millennium of the Church's presence on Polish territory thousands of churches, monasteries and chapels were erected, in which the Catholic population could worship God, thereby confirming its adherence to Christendom. Not much has come down to our times of the most ancient, modest Romanesque churches going back to the 11th or 12th centuries. Most of them perished, too humble, too small to accommodate the ever growing congregations. Upon their foundations there shot up into the sky the proud pointed Gothic edifices, some of them rivalling their famous European counterparts in size. These relics of the original churches are of colossal importance, however, since they also mark the spiritual origins of the Church in Poland. Polish churches have always been beautiful and original, embellished and enriched by signally indigenous elements. They would be built by first-rate masters, both local men and foreigners, who would come at the invitation of mighty patrons – kings, lords, patricians, monastic communities. Poland must have been an attractive place for church builders, if such masterpieces unparalleled elsewhere in medieval Europe were created here.

The most brilliant specimen of religious art was made for St. Mary's Basilica of Cracow, by Veit Stoss, master sculptor of Nuremberg. The central panel of his famous late 15th-century altar shows the scene of the Dormition, in which the Virgin swoons into the arms of the Apostles. The panels and wings of the pentaptych present other scenes from the life and passion of Jesus, and the life of Mary. Their stories combine in this masterpiece and culminate in Mary's coronation in Heaven, giving the quintessence of Polish Catholicism as it has persisted over the ages and as it is now – very much alive.

The magnificent Polish churches created in the diverse ages in a variety of styles are so numerous throughout the entire country that it would be impossible to list them all. They include absolute gems of art and architecture like Dębno Church in the Podhale, one of the oldest in its kind, going back to the 15th century. The colourful stencilled decorations painted on its walls, ceiling, and furnishings, along with its original altar endow this church with a singular charm. Another masterpiece on the global scale is the late 19th-century subterranean Chapel of St. Kinga in the depths of Wieliczka Salt Mine. The bas-reliefs, floors, chandeliers, and saints' statues in it were all carved by artists who were miners by profession.

A land of spontaneous, ardent religious piety, Poland is full of places of worship, not only Roman Catholic ones. The religious tolerance which for many centuries was a special distinguishing feature of this country's home policy, allowed its people to worship and raise their houses of prayer as they pleased. Hence, side by side with the Roman Catholic churches, in Poland you will also find Eastern-rite churches, both Uniate and Orthodox; Protestant churches; Jewish synagogues; and the mosques of the Polish Tartars. They are all associated with the turbulent and glorious history of this land and the peoples inhabiting it. Together they all give a unique account of ten centuries of the development of art in its successive styles, its changing vogues, the invariably high quality of the work done by the master artists, builders, painters, sculptors, stucco-artists, joiners, organ-makers and stained-glass window-makers who flourished here.

In the east of Poland Christianity of the Byzantine rite took root. In the Union of Brześć of 1596 its clergy acknowledged the ecclesiastical supremacy of Rome but retained its Eastern rite. The exquisitely beautiful Eastern-rite Russniak and Ukrainian churches of southern and eastern Poland are an inseparable component of the Carpathian countryside. Their unique architecture comprises a collectively wrought work of art out of the local building traditions using wood, through individual contributions by master joiners and church painters. One of the most beautiful is Powroźnik Church, an early 17th-century example, but its junior counterparts, mostly 19th-century, are also fine specimens of their kind.

Since the Middle Ages Poland, and especially its towns, provided a favourite place of settlement for the Jews, who fled Western Europe on account of the pogroms there. The country's prosperity gave them better prospects both of economic advancement and peaceful existence. An expression of this state of affairs are the splendid and well-constructed synagogues built here over the centuries. Although the

religious tradition was different, the building methods used to put up the Jewish prayer-houses relied on the local techniques and traditions. The brickbuilt Renaissance synagogues of Cracow, Zamość and Łańcut are reminiscent of the Polish fortified *dwór*, and their attics are decorated like the Cracovian town houses. The wooden synagogues, which alas fell victim to the Holocaust, had mighty mansard-type roofs jutting out into the local skyline and were similar in structure to the wooden alcoved *dwory*. The synagogue at Tykocin, in eastern Poland, is just such a fine example of the local Jewish tradition in religious building.

The Protestant (Lutheran) churches, which are to be found especially in the western and northern parts of Poland, were also grounded in the local tradition in architecture. The Peace Churches at Świdnica and Jawor, erected in the mid-17th century, were built by the same master craftsmen who made the Catholic religious works of art of Lower Silesia. These monumental structures are so beautiful and perfect down to the smallest detail that it is hard to believe that the local Lutheran congregations were allowed just one year to build them by the ruling Habsburgs, who thought this would be a good way to humiliate their Protestant subjects. Our religious mosaic would not be complete if we missed the Polish Tartars' mosques, or the *molenna*

prayer-houses of the Old Believers, who migrated to Poland to escape persecution in Russia. Only in Poland could they live in peace side by side with the Orthodox Christians, who also raised many fine Orthodox churches, such as Jabłeczna Church, decorated in the Great Russian style.

Finally Poland, just like many other countries throughout the world, has its special places of worship where religious devotion still continues to be paid, just as it has always done. Each region of Poland has its religious sanctuaries, which draw in streams of pilgrims. Góra Świętej Anny (St. Anne's Mountain), Święta Lipka, Kalwaria Zebrzydowska, and Grabarka Mountain for Orthodox Christians, and many, many more places of pilgrimage have over the centuries been made sacred by the deep faith of innumerable generations. The principal shrine for religious piety is Jasna Góra (Mons Clarus, Bright Mountain) at Częstochowa, sanctuary of the Black Madonna, Queen of Poland.

Wawel Cathedral, Cracow, with the royal chapels of the Jagiellonian and Vasa dynasties

208

Main nave of Wawel
Cathedral with the
Confession of St.
Stanislaus, Bishop
and Martyr, slain at
the behest of King
Boleslaus the Bold
in the 11th century

209

Pauline Church and Monastery at Skałka, Cracow, where St. Stanislaus was martyred. To commemorate these events, every year in May a procession leaves from Wawel Cathedral to Skałka Church with the Saint's relics, and returns after an open-air Mass

Gniezno Cathedral, containing the relics of St. Adalbert, Bishop of Prague, killed by pagans in the 10th century during a missionary expedition. Today St. Adalbert is a symbol of the unity of the nations of Central and Eastern Europe

The High Altar of
St. Mary's Basilica,
Cracow, with a scene
of the Dormition of
the Virgin Mary in
its central panel.
This pentaptych was
made by Veit Stoss of
Nuremberg in the latter
half of the 15th century
for this church in
Cracow

Wrocław Cathedral, raised on Ostrów Tumski (Cathedral Island), the oldest part of the city. The Gothic cathedral was erected at the turn of the 13th and 14th centuries on the site of previous churches, which stood here from 1000 onwards, when the bishopric was founded.

Płock Cathedral and its close, a Romanesque group. It stands on a cliff overlooking the Vistula with a marvellous view of the river and the Mazovian countryside, which in the 11th century was put under the spiritual authority of the Bishop of Płock

215

Romanesque Cathedral
of the Blessed Virgin
Mary, at Oliwa,
Gdańsk. This cathedral
is located in the
grounds of a former
Cistercian abbey, and
it has an appended,
exquisitely adapted
Rococo façade

The organ of Oliwa Cathedral, one of the finest instruments in its class in Europe. It took over twenty years to construct it in the second half of the 18th century; the work was started by Johannes Wulf of Orneta, and completed by Friedrich Rudolf Dalitz, organ-master of Gdańsk

Interior of the
Cathedral of the
Blessed Virgin Mary,
Pelplin, situated in
a former Cistercian
abbey. Pelplin
Cathedral, a mighty
14th-century structure,
is one of the finest
specimens of Gothic
church architecture
in Poland

219

Shrine of Our Lady of Święta Lipka, the principal pilgrimage centre in Varmia and Masuria. The Baroque monastic buildings were erected for the Jesuits in the 17th century, and extended in the next century to include the place which for centuries had been associated with the veneration of a holy statue of the Virgin

Former Camaldolese hermitage on Lake Wigry in the Augustów Lake District. Camaldolese hermits always selected beautiful spots for their abodes, good for a life of contemplation

Observantine Priory at Kalwaria Zebrzydowska. The Priory and the surrounding open-air calvary *(via dolorosa)* were founded by Mikołaj Zebrzydowski in the early 17th century

The Pauline Monastery of Jasna Góra was founded in the 14th century for a new order which came to Poland from Hungary. Its bastioned fortifications withstood the Swedish siege in 1655. The event was ascribed to a miracle wrought by the holy image of Our Lady of Częstochowa, which is preserved here by the Pauline Order

Camaldolese
Hermitage at Bielany
near Cracow, founded
in the early 17th
century by Mikołaj
Wolski, Lord Grand
Marshal of the Realm

Tyniec Benedictine
Abbey near Cracow,
one of the oldest
religious foundations
in Poland, founded in
the 11th century,
probably by King
Boleslaus the Bold

Przemyśl Cathedral. Its interior is a combination of a Gothic structure with Baroque decorations – a phenomenon typical of Polish churches

15th-century Dębno Church in the Podhale region, one of the oldest, and certainly the most beautiful of Poland's extant wooden churches

Late Gothic stencilled
polychromy in Dębno
Church in the Podhale

Jawor Lutheran Church, one of the three wooden Protestant Peace Churches built in the mid 17th century in Lower Silesia to mark the Peace of Westphalia after the Thirty Years' War

The Holy Picture of
Our Lady of Kodeń,
Queen of Podlassia.
On praying before thi
image in the Vatican,
the Polish lord Mikoła
Sapieha is said to
have recovered
his health.
He subsequently
stole the holy picture
and brought it to
Kodeń. The holy
image is venerated
both by the Roman
and Uniate Catholics
of Podlassia

Interior of Tykocin
Synagogue
(17th-century),
one of the finest extant
synagogues in Poland,
now housing
a museum of Judaism

237

Wooden chapel in the grounds of the Orthodox Monastery of St. Onophrios at Jabłeczna in Podlassia a well-known place of pilgrimage

Kruszyniany Mosque in the region of Białystok, used by the Polish Tartars. Built in the mid-19th century for a Polish Muslim community, its shape is reminiscent of the wooden Christian churches of the neighbourhood

Mass for St. Barbara's Day in the Chapel of St. Kinga in the Wieliczka Salt Mine, a unique heritage site. The chapel was made in the 19th century in a disused chamber in the mine, and most of the decoration, sculptures, and bas-reliefs were made in rock salt by local miners who were amateur artists

241

Graves

On the first night of November, usually already a cold night, a glowing arc of light shines over the graveyards, cemeteries and burial places in the cities, towns, and villages of Poland. It comes from millions of graveside lamps and candles lit on that day on family graves and in the places where the heroes of the wars and national uprisings have been laid to rest. There is a smell of melting wax, flowers and pine needles in the air. In his book on cemeteries Jacek Kolbuszewski writes, 'Each human presence at a dear person's graveside is a demonstrative, albeit usually not at all ostentatious, sign that those who have departed are still remembered... The graveyard is a place of remembrance.' 'Nations which lose their remembrance lose their lives,' reads the inscription over the old graveyard at Zakopane. Until the close of the 18th century burials were made in church crypts or churchyards, and

these places were treated as integral parts of the place of worship. They were sacred. The dead were where they had spent their lives: within the city walls. Only the Jewish communities would bury their dead in a graveyard which was removed from the synagogue and from their houses, usually on a hillside, so that the deceased could look out towards the Promised Land which they did not manage to reach during their lifetimes. Otherwise burial sites beyond the municipal boundaries would be for the victims of epidemics and for those who were denied interment in hallowed ground by Canon Law. But people tended not to speak about these places. That is why, when new burial grounds were first established outside the municipal areas, at the turn of the 18th and 19th centuries, they did not meet with public approval straightaway. Gradually, however, the new custom was accepted and its advantages recognised.

Unlike the churchyards, in which new interments would be made into previously occupied graves, these new 'general' foundations gave the feeling of permanence, and hence the desire to put up an impressive monument for a tombstone. Soon after the establishment of the first extra-municipal cemeteries – the Powązkowski in Warsaw, 1790, and the Rakowicki in Cracow at the turn of the 19th century – the art of graveside memorials started devel-

oping on a tremendous scale. The parkland settings of the new cemeteries would be designed by outstanding architects, and the best sculptors would be employed to make the memorials. The first-rate work they created would then serve as models for the humbler stonemasons. Some of their not very successful or naïve imitations might perhaps look slightly ridiculous, but they are nevertheless testimonies of remembrance. Under the Partitions the nation's cemeteries offered an unprecedented place for the expression of forbidden longing for freedom and independence. Here respect could be paid to those who had fallen in the national uprisings, to the victims of oppression by the partitioning powers, to deceased individuals known for their intransigent spirit. An appropriately arranged graveside memorial could give expression to what it was forbidden by the censors to say or write. Hence the multiplicity of the symbols: the eagle about to spread its wings; figures tearing off their chains; the arms of Poland, Lithuania, and Ruthenia. Epitaphs would use cryptic language to say that the deceased had taken part in an uprising or been deported to Siberia, or suffered persecution.

The dead, and especially those who had fallen in the uprisings, would be interred in an atmosphere of truly royal pomp and ceremony, in appropriately stately burial places.

The proximity of the royal burial crypt in Wawel Cathedral, a place all Polish people held sacred since it was a symbol of their country's liberty and indomitable spirit, certainly left its mark on the development of Rakowice Cemetery in Cracow. Apart from the kings and queens of Poland, who had been interred at Wawel centuries ago, the Cathedral was also the place where the mortal remains of the national heroes, Prince Józef Poniatowski and Tadeusz Kościuszko, had been laid to rest in funeral processions that had occasioned the public expression of patriotic feelings. Later General Piłsudski, and recently also General Sikorski, were honoured by burial at Wawel.

Eventually burial in Rakowice Cemetery, so near Wawel Hill, became something of a status symbol, and in the 19th century Stanisław Estreicher wrote that Cracow was the heart and sanctuary of Poland, to which all the great came in their old age to 'lay their bones at the foot of Wawel Hill.'

Near Wawel, at Skałka Church, yet another place of remembrance was set up in honour of the greatest who had contributed to the growth of the Polish national spirit, especially in the arts and sciences. Jan Długosz, 15th-century chronicler of medieval Poland and tutor to the king's sons, lies here; alongside the poet Wincenty Pol, the painter Henryk Siemiradzki, and the painter and dramatist Stanisław Wyspiański. The painter Jan Matejko is buried in his family tomb at Rakowice, in accordance with his last will.

The Powązkowski Cemetery in Warsaw, one of the largest burial grounds in Europe, is a veritable treasury of sculpture. It commemorates Poland's bitterest moments of the past century. Here, under a sweep of stone and silver-birch crosses, sleep the young combatants of the 1944 Warsaw Uprising. Here for many years the Polish officers murdered by the Soviets in the Katyn Massacre were clandestinely honoured when officially it was forbidden to keep their memory alive. The flowers and candles put in a special spot tacitly set aside for them symbolised the spirit and desire of independence in the same way as a century earlier the flowers of insurgents' graves had done.

The bond between the quick and the dead is more than a bond in the family and nation. Religion plays a signal role in this aspect of life, and in the denominational cemeteries which were the predominant type of cemeteries in Poland up to the 20th century religion was the decisive factor determining the spatial arrangement, the type of memorials, and the gestures of remembrance used. There were Orthodox Christian cemeteries in Poland, and there were also Jewish cemeteries, few of which were left after the devastation of the Second World War, and there were Protestant cemeteries. All of them were part of the Polish landscape, reminders that the country was a mosaic of religions and cultures which over the centuries had contributed to the nation's joint heritage.

Burial grounds comprise a world dedicated to the past. They are *necropoleis*, cities of the dead, touching and nostalgic, symbols of history, both national and personal, the frontier between the worlds, testimonies of union with the land, with one's native land. Burial grounds remind the living of the inexorable passing of time, but also of the salutary role of remembrance. The Latin adage, *Quod sum eris; quod es antea fui* (What I am you will be; what you are I was once) should perhaps be supplemented by another saying, 'Lest we forget.'

St. Leonard's Crypt, a surviving part of the oldest cathedral church on Wawel Hill, including the tomb of Bishop Maurus below floor level. The Crypt also contains the tombs of King John III Sobieski and his French consort, Marie Casimire d'Arquien, of King Michał Korybut Wiśniowiecki, Prince Józef Poniatowski, Tadeusz Kościuszko, and General Sikorski

The Poets' Crypt in
Wawel Cathedral,
with the tombs of
Adam Mickiewicz
and Juliusz Słowacki.
The mortal remains of
Poland's greatest poets
were brought here
from Paris in 1890
and 1927 respectively

The old part of the Powązkowski Cemetery, founded in 1790 as one of Poland's first municipal cemeteries located beyond the city boundaries

Family tomb of the
painter Jan Matejko
in the Rakowicki
Cemetery, Cracow

Tombstones in the derelict and devastated Jewish Cemetery at Lubaczów. Before the Second World War Jews made up a substantial part of the inhabitants of Poland's towns and cities. Their cemeteries and synagogues are what has remained of those times

Churchyard of the
mid-17th century
Protestant Peace
Church at Świdnica

Russniak graveside
memorials in the
churchyard at
Hańczowa in the
Beskidy Mountains

Churchyard of Opaka
Ukrainian Church in
the region of Rzeszów

Monumental tombstones in the Ukrainian churchyard in the village of Paździacz near Przemyśl. The Beskidy mountain area was famous for its stonemasons, who made innumerable roadside crosses and holy statutes, as well as tombstones with images of the Virgin Mary or of the Risen Christ

Crypt of Marshal Józe[f]
Piłsudski, creator of th[e]
modern independent
state of Poland.
The crypt is located
under the Tower
of the Silver Bells in
Wawel Cathedral

Monument of the Victims of Communism in the Rakowicki Cemetery, Cracow. The cross symbolises faith, which during the years of Communist terror and oppression was often the only haven of safety available

Silver birch crosses on the graves of the Warsaw Insurgents of 1944, in the military section of the Powązkowski Cemetery

The Katyn memorial precinct in the military section of the Powązkowski Cemetery. For half a century this spot served as the symbolic collective grave of the Polish officers who had been murdered by the NKVD

BOSZ
38-622 Olszanica 311; Biuro: 38-600 Lesko, ul. Parkowa 5
tel. +48 (13) 4699000, fax +48 (13) 4696188
e-mail: biuro@bosz.com.pl
www.bosz.com.pl